THE ROAD TO HELL:
RECOLLECTIONS OF THE NAZI DEATH MARCH

THE ROAD TO HELL:

RECOLLECTIONS OF THE NAZI DEATH MARCH

by

JOSEPH FREEMAN
AND
DONALD SCHWARTZ

PARAGON HOUSE
St. Paul, Minnesota

Published in the United States by

Paragon House
2700 University Avenue West
St. Paul, Minnesota 55114

Cover photo courtesy of United States Holocaust Memorial Museum photo
archives © Dachau concentration camp memorial site—archives.

Library of Congress Catalog-in-Publication Data

Freeman, Joseph, 1915-
      The road to hell: recollections of the Nazi death march / by Joseph
  Freeman; edited by Donald Schwartz
        p.   cm.
    ISBN: 1-55778-762-X (pbk.)
    1. Freeman, Joseph, 1915-   2. Holocaust, Jewish)1939-1945)
  —Germany—Personal narratives. 3. Death marches—Germany.
  I. Schwartz, Donald R. (Donald Robert), 1943- . II. Title.
    D804.7.D43F64   1998
    940.53'18'0943—dc21   97-33063
                                          CIP

Contents

Preface

My first book took six years to write. With the completion of *Job: The Story of a Holocaust Survivor*, I thought that I was leaving behind my horrible past, so full of pain and suffering. In it I shared with you, dear reader, how a young man—a Jew—went through the Nazi Hell, how the belief in the Almighty and the power of love kept him alive, and how moral strength helped him to overcome the Angel of Death.

It is the story of a struggle between the modern Job and the Devil, and how I came back from the dead. If you read the book you shared my torment under Nazi oppression as well as the delirious moment of my liberation. You were with me as I met my dream girl, Helen, who also miraculously survived the Holocaust. You read how I started a new life, first in postwar Germany on the soil soaked with the blood of my loved ones. At the end of the book you came with me to this wonderful United States where I started to build a future for me and my family. You were with me in my struggles, my peaks and valleys. You relived with me my meeting with Professor Elie Wiesel, the man who inspired me, who guided me with his teaching. This was the man who showed me my destiny. With his encouragement, I left the business world and went back to study, to catch up with my past. I entered the world of knowledge, devoting twelve years to study about what happened when I was confined like an animal in the death camps.

The years have been going by too quickly. I took the torch of remembrance, teaching and sharing with people of all races and religions what bigotry and hate can do. You saw how I grappled with the impossible task of writing my life story and how I suffered reliving my terrifying past. But as I read and re-read that manuscript, I realized that the book was incomplete. Missing were the six weeks when I was on the Death March prior to liberation. Why had I obliterated this memory? Unconsciously I was trying to erase the anguish of that experience, a trauma so deep and terrifying that I needed time to come to terms with my past. I struggled to recall what happened during those six weeks as I started to write this book. I remembered only bits and pieces but then slowly the incidents came back to me. As more and more events flooded my memory I was left crying, reliving a time when tens of thousands had been slaughtered by the SS, or had died from cold or starvation. Even now my stomach turns as I recall how the so-called 'master race' behaved in the last days of the war, how they killed helpless sick people and how they reacted when the liberators approached.

I knew when I sat down to put this remembrance on paper that I would go through Hell again reliving the inhumane suffering, but I had to do it. The hour is growing late, the years in front of me are diminishing. I feel it is the duty of survivors to recall the horror, the misery and torment to remind the reading public of what brutalities the human species is capable of, in hope of preventing such a catastrophe from ever happening again. Over the past ten years I have traveled the world with my wife, Helen, to share with others our experiences in the time of "Doom." I have produced thirty movies and videos on the subject of the Holocaust. There is still so much to learn. The collapse of the Soviet Union has made available a rich archive of new material about the Nazis and the occupation of Russia.

I'm happy that I have chosen the road to which Professor Wiesel led me. I hope my books and films will serve as a testimony to future generations so they will not forget what happened before they were born, so they will remember the lessons of the most terrible chapter of the twentieth century.

Dedication and Acknowledgments

This book is dedicated to the hundreds of thousands of young men and women of Jewish faith and ten thousand others who perished on the road to Germany from January 1st until April 26th, 1945. They are the unknown victims and unknown heroes who perished at the hands of the Nazis. The SS continued its murderous rampage until the last day, to the last hour of the war. This book describes the experiences of one of the very few who survived the death march.

I wish to thank Professor Donald Schwartz for his advice and encouragement in writing this book. I also want to express my deep appreciation to Professor John Roth, without whose guidance and remarks this book would never have been completed. Last but not least, my gratitude goes to my lovely wife, Helen, who was so patient as I took time away from our normal routine, time which is so irreplaceable at this stage in our lives.

Map Of The Death March

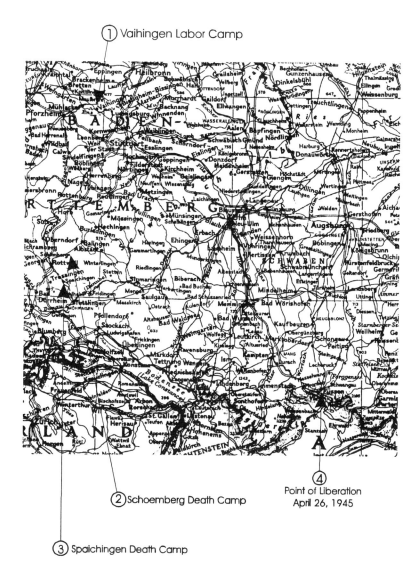

① Vaihingen Labor Camp

② Schoemberg Death Camp

④ Point of Liberation
April 26, 1945

③ Spaichingen Death Camp

The Death March from March 16 to April 26, 1945 began at Spaichingen Death Camp and ended approximately 100 miles away near Fussen.

Introduction

In the last few months of World War II Soviet armies advanced in the east while American, British and French forces pressed Germany in the west. In response to these offensives, the Nazis decided to evacuate and dismantle concentration camps hoping to conceal their heinous crimes. That process actually began in the summer of 1944 when evacuations began at Auschwitz, the largest of the concentration camps. The Germans finally liquidated that killing center in mid-January 1945, forcing some sixty-six thousand prisoners to take to the roads. The following month the camp at Gross Rosen, with its forty thousand prisoners, was evacuated. With Allied forces closing in, the Germans emptied one camp after another. The massive transfer of hundreds of thousands of sickly and emaciated inmates became known as the 'death marches', in reference to the enormous number of fatalities resulting from the ordeal.

When that evacuations began, there were some seven hundred thousand prisoners in concentration camps throughout Europe, run by approximately forty thousand SS guards and administrators. It has been estimated that almost a quarter of a million camp inmates died in forced marches across central Europe from January to May, 1945. The evacuations occurred in camps throughout German occupied territories, and everywhere the camp population was brutalized and tormented. Ill-clad, they froze in sub-zero temperatures; exhausted, they received little more than stale bread and water for their daily rations. Not surprisingly, many prisoners succumbed to the bitter cold, to hunger, or to the effects of typhus. But a staggering number of victims died from brutal abuse and outright murder at the hands of their guards. Many were shot or beaten to death because they were too weak to keep pace, or because they had fallen down. Victims included women as well as men, Gypsies, homosexuals, Jehovah Witnesses, Soviet prisoners-of-war as well as Spanish republicans, although Jews accounted for at least half the number of fatalities. The persecution continued even as the Third Reich crumbled, even after Hitler's suicide on April 30th. Ironically, the last death march began on May 7th, the same day that Germany surrendered to the Allies.

There is some debate about the origins of this final chapter in the 'Final Solution.' There is no evidence of an official order calling for the murder of evacuated inmates. Most likely the massacres resulted from numerous factors, not the least of which was the chaos attending the end of the war. Some of the killers may have been true believers in Nazi ideology, convinced that every last Jew remained an enemy and a threat to the Third Reich. To be sure, the Nazis accelerated the mass extermination of Jews in the final months of the war, and the shooting of prisoners on the death marches may have been an unstated corollary to that policy. Undoubtedly, some SS officers regarded the executions as an extension of the practice of eliminating those prisoners incapable of caring for themselves; others may have shot the marchers to prevent them from reporting the brutalities to the liberating Allied armies.

Interestingly, little has been written about this horrifying and catastrophic episode, perhaps because so few survived the ordeal, and perhaps because those who did tried to obliterate the terror from their memories. On March 16, 1945, the Germans liquidated the camp at Spaichingen, located in southwestern Germany, about twenty miles north of the Swiss border. Joseph Freeman and thousands of other inmates began a six-week ordeal that ended in the city of Fussen in southern Germany. Freeman omitted reference to the death march in his first book, *Job: The Story of a Holocaust Survivor*, because he could not face the trauma of recollection. But after completing that work, images and episodes of the death march long forgotten began to emerge in his consciousness. The deprivations he and his comrades were forced to endure are almost unimaginable; nevertheless, he felt compelled to record the horror so that the world would never forget; on a personal level he wrote this book because he felt the need to fill in the missing pages of his life. In the course of his writing he had to confront a past he had blocked out for some fifty years. Recalling the excruciatingly painful memories left him wreaked with anxiety, to the point that he could not sleep for weeks. He suffered a nervous trauma that left him temporarily deaf. Nevertheless, he persisted, driven by the need to inform present and future generations what he and his co-religionists were forced to endure. This book is a testimony to Joseph Freeman's indomitable spirit and his devotion to his life's mission: to guarantee that such atrocities will never again be tolerated by civilized society.

Donald Schwartz, Ph.D.
California State University, Long Beach

PART ONE

The Preparation For Hell

Chapter One

To Spaichingen:
A New Place of Misery

On the eve of World War II I had been admitted to a medical school in Warsaw. But with the Nazi conquest of Poland my life was turned upside down. As a Jew, I was considered unfit to live. Consequently, I spent the war years in a series of ghettos, labor camps, and death camps. I cannot fully explain how I managed to survive; my guardian angel must have been watching over me.

From 1939 to 1944 I was assigned to several different work camps (Arbeitslager) in German-occupied Poland. In July 1944, I was sent to Auschwitz, where from the railroad car I witnessed the deadly selection process. Fortunately, I was not destined for the concentration camp at Auschwitz; rather, I was in a cattle train and transported to Veihingen, a labor camp in Germany located twenty miles north of Stuttgart. After three months of back-breaking work, I was sent to a death camp in Schoemberg, some fifty miles south of Veihingen.

In Schoemberg I worked in the camp infirmary but I was not prepared to take charge of a hospital with thousands of dying inmates. Nevertheless the Lagerfuehrer insisted that I tend to the sick and he would have killed me had I refused. To make matters worse, the SS forced me to administer my medical skills, not to sustain life but rather to prolong the suffering of the poor wretches too weak to rise from their beds. The hospital was a medical facility in name only. Actually, it was a way station where people came to die, not to regain their health. In the short few months that I worked there I witnessed the death of thousands. Not a single patient recovered from his illness, and most expired within two weeks. I remember the faces of the young men begging for me to help them. Their voices still ring in my ears. They had been dying in my arms. They were too young to die. What could I do for them? I could only try to comfort them, wash their young faces, and pray with them. But I knew prayers could not help; as a doctor I needed medication and antibiotics, supplicants which were unavailable to me. Nevertheless, I risked my life to help these suffering inmates. There were few medical supplies in the facility, so at night I took the bedsheets and ripped them into pieces and washed them for later use as bandages. This constituted an act of sabotage, so I had to be particularly careful to replace the missing sheets. I explained to the camp officials that nurses used sheets to cover the dead, whose clothes had been removed and recycled to other inmates.

But the experience exacted a terrible toll on me. Despite working hard all day, I found it impossible to sleep at night. The moment I closed my eyes I was confronted by the faces of the dying people. I was haunted by their pleading eyes and their mournful cries for help. The voices of the dying followed me everywhere. I lost my appetite and I became sick. Constantly exposed to pain and suffering, I became immersed in a depression that almost drove me insane. I had to find a way out of the slaughterhouse that passed for a camp clinic. The death of my close friend Wladek brought me to my physical and psychological breaking point. This loss was the final straw; I could not take anymore of being close to someone who would soon die. I bribed a Kapo to get me on a list for a transport leaving for Spaichingen, another death camp some thirty miles to the south. I could only thank the Almighty that I was finally leaving the Schoemberg concentration camp.

I arrived at Spaichingen along with other inmates packed into the back of an army truck. When we passed through the camp entrance the SS ordered us out of the truck. No sooner had we left the vehicle when sirens sounded an air raid. Aircraft flying at tremendous speed were headed in our direction. We scrambled to find shelter. Shortly, the alarm ended. Kapos from the new camp directed us to the bath house where we shaved and showered. We were issued new clothes and a new pair of shoes. It was the first time in months that I was given a new pair of underwear. Smaller than Schoemberg, the camp consisted of only nine barracks housing two hundred and fifty inmates in each. I was assigned to Barracks 3. Entering the barracks, I saw a face from the past. I had sold him some books after my graduation from gymnasium, and he had visited my house on several occasions. I remembered his name—Chaim Schluftman. At first he did not respond when I called out to him. "Chaim, do you remember me? I'm Joseph Friedman from Radom. You had a friend named Moniek Rubinstein. Do you remember me now?" He stared at me with a curious gaze, shook his arms and then excitedly he shouted, "Oh yes, I remember you. Josek Friedman from Radom. You lived on Zeromskiego Street, yes? Tania was your sister's name."

Crying, we embraced each other. After so many months in a place of death, I had found a friend. I was not alone anymore. We sat and talked for hours, recalling our past. I told him how I lost my family, recounting the time of the liquidation of our ghetto in Radom, and the tragic moment of losing my father and mother. I recounted the devastating moment when during a Nazi Aktion I directed my sister Tania to stand by my mother and to stay with her. Chaim interrupted me as I was telling him that with my own hands I unwittingly sent my sister to her death. "Josek, you were not to blame. We did not know what we were doing. The Germans had been telling us lies, constantly, saying they were sending our people to the east and that they would care for them. In the beginning we believed them until we found out the truth. Then it was too late. You cannot blame yourself. I, too, lived through a similar moment of desperation. I did not know how to behave. We had lost ourselves in that tragic moment. They took away from us the will to live and to act. We were helpless, facing the cruelty of the Germans. We were not prepared to fight a system based on lies. I, too, have suffered like you. My family was killed. Like you, I'm the only one from my family still alive. But I don't give up hope. Remember, some of us have to survive to tell the world the truth."

Chaim gave me the courage not to give in. We shared stories of our recent experiences. I told him of the pain and suffering at the Schoemberg hospital and how I lost my friend Wladek. Chaim had been on the road for months in custody of SS guards who were retreating before the rapid advance of the Soviet army. He wandered from one camp to another until he reached Spaichingen several months prior to my arrival there. As I listened to him I was astonished at his determination to survive and endure living through this hell. I was broken physically and mentally; the loss of my loved ones had touched me so deeply that I had lost the will to fight. After recounting our sad remembrances we quietly sobbed, shaking our heads. What else could we do, sharing a past so full of torment.

I awoke the next morning in my new place of misery. Yet I thanked the Almighty that I did not have to return to the Schoemberg hospital. The Kapos ordered us to stand in front of our barracks for Appel, the counting time. We stood in groups of one hundred, a Kapo in front. Silent, we stood and waited. A whistle. The *Lagerfuehrer* approached with a group of SS following close behind. Paper and pencil in hand, the Lagerfuehrer passed by each group, counting, making marks on his papers. After one hour, it was over. Luckily, that morning not too many had been sick. Those who could not get out of bed had been taken to the hospital before the counting time and their presence was accounted for. German punctuality. German orderliness. The number of inmates standing for Appel had to match the numbers from the camp headquarters. If not, we would have to stand for hours until the missing prisoner was found. Dead or alive, it didn't matter to the Germans, as long as the numbers matched. Sometimes it took hours to account for the missing. During that time the prisoners had to stand and wait. Rain or cold, the camp officials did not care. Fortunately, this particular morning everything went smoothly.

A whistle sounded and we moved to our eating place. Hungry, standing in line, we waited for the sound of the whistle signaling us to begin eating. No talking. The SS guarded the line from both sides, watching us so that we stayed in order. When someone even slightly moved out, he was hit with a bamboo stick. It was not easy to stand and watch, but we did not have any choice. Finally, the whistle blew. We had to move fast, getting our ration which consisted of a small piece of bread and a cup of warm black solution which was supposed to be coffee. Getting our food, we had to eat fast and move toward the direction of the camp gate. A Kapo headed each group of one hundred passing through the gate. The Lagerelder carefully counted each inmate. Once through the gate, the SS took over, surrounding us on both sides. Some of the guards had German shepherds on leashes.

Our work was different than in Schoemberg. The camp was located near the city of Spaichingen. Sometimes we were taken to the city by truck to clean up debris from houses destroyed by American bombers. For the first time we saw Germans crying over the destruction of their homes. This was the first time I had seen a German shed tears. I felt sorry that civilians had to suffer, but I reveled in the satisfaction that I survived long enough to see Germans pay a price for the pain and suffering that so many of us had to endure. While cleaning up the rubbish we found plenty of food which we ate quickly, lest the SS found out. After clearing the wreckage and ruins, we were ordered to build barracks to serve as temporary housing for the displaced Germans. It was not easy work, but I felt lucky to be in Spaichingen. I became accustomed to the routine and I didn't have to deal with the horrors that I encountered at Schoemberg. But all this changed after two weeks. The SS men were replaced by a new cadre of SS who behaved very cruelly. They had come from the Russian front where they had experienced the most brutal ravages of combat. Now they took out their anger and frustration on helpless camp prisoners. We had to work constantly. No time for rest. No more driving to work; we had to walk in a straight line with no talking. Inmates who strayed from the line were smashed by the butt of the SS man's rifle. Our new guards addressed us as *Schmutzige Jude* (filthy Jews). We were dehumanized, robbed of dignity and sense of worth. I had been in Spaichingen for a month and it felt like a lifetime.

Chapter Two

The Night Before The March
March 15, 1945

It was still dark outside. The silence was only interrupted by the voices of the SS talking to one another as they walked around the fences of the camp, watching us behind the confines of the barracks. Not a soul was moving. The guards had orders to shoot any moving object. These were strict orders. We knew this. We stayed in the barracks. We only moved on the Kapos orders. The compound was quiet; only the snoring of some sleeping inmates interrupted the silence. The lamp over the table in the middle of the barracks was still burning. Nevertheless, it was dark, you could hardly see. Then the stillness was disturbed by noise coming from the Kapo's room. We knew what was going on. The Kapo was the master of our lives and he took advantage of his power. He chose two young boys from our barracks. He protected these youths and gave them extra food. They did not go out to work. Their job was to take care of the inside of the barracks—cleaning, removing the sick, and to be sure that before leaving we put in order the blankets which covered our wooden beds. The chosen boys slept in his room. Our Kapo was a homosexual. We had known this. He was a German with special privileges. A political disagreement with a Nazi captor put him in this place. He wore a red square on his uniform. This insignia distinguished him from other inmates. He was strong and tall, over six feet in height. Every two weeks he received some packages from his family, mostly cigarettes, which he would exchange for money or jewelry with inmates in the barracks. Exchanging was the job of the two young boys. They got food and clothing for the service and they had been doing a good job for their master.

I could not sleep. Lying on my bed, I turned from one side to the other. My friend, Chaim, was asleep. Yesterday we worked hard, finishing the road in front of the main entrance to the camp. For weeks we had been cleaning. We worked from 8:00 in the morning, sweeping the barracks, removing debris and leaves, piling them in one place, then moving them by wheelbarrows to the gate. From there another group of inmates loaded the refuse onto a truck. Now came the hard part. We had to remove the stones which were lying around half frozen to the ground. First we had to dig them out with picks and shovels, then with our bare hands we had to pick up the stones and put them in wheelbarrows which another group of inmates moved to the fence around the camp. This was March 1945, in Germany. It was very cold. It was painful to pick up the icy stones with our bare hands. After a short time the frigid stones stuck to our hands which became swollen. We could not stop. Some of us began to cry. The Kapo rushed us to work faster but it was impossible. The pain was becoming too much to bear. The SS stood around us, hollering, calling in German, "Macht schnell" (move fast). Tears were running down the faces of my fellow prisoners.

We worked until the sound of the whistle was heard. This was the signal for us to stop. It was already 5:00 in the evening. Exhausted, hungry, still we had to follow the orders of the Kapo. We did not know that this was our last day in this place of misery. Later that night Chaim turned in his bed, awakening me. I lifted my head and looked around. It was growing light outside, the beginning of another day. At that moment, I felt grateful to be alive. I recalled the words of my friend, Rabbi Lester, who said to me, "Joseph, so long as you are alive, you will have hope. Believe in the Almighty and He will help you. Remember, we are not forgotten." Oh, how I miss him. He gave me courage to believe in a tomorrow that did not exist in the Schoemberg Death Camp.

At this moment I feel terrible, recalling my past. It was so long ago. But for me it is as though it only happened a few hours ago. For two years I thought of writing about my terrible time in the last months of the Death March before I was ready to sit down and put my feelings and thoughts on paper. It is not easy for me to recall the tragic moments during which I was dying from hunger and sickness. It is impossible to fully understand how I survived. Fifty years later the voices of my friends are ringing in my ears, calling for mercy as the SS were shooting the sick and the lame. These awful memories will stay with me for as long as I live. When these events happened each moment was an eternity, full of suffering. I am shaking as I recall the horrors of my past. It was so many years ago. We survivors have to live with our past, with the pain of remembering, to inform others of what happened before they were born. We remember so that we can function as normal people wherever we are.

Chapter Three

The Last Morning Before The Death March

Early on March 16, 1945, the doors to our barracks had been forced open and the SS rushed in shouting in German, "Raus, Raus!" Frightened, we jumped quickly from our bunks, hurriedly putting on our clothes. My friend, Chaim, was already out of bed, almost completely dressed. In seconds, we straightened out our beds and covered them with blankets. We ran outside and waited for our orders. What next? It was unusual that it was the SS rather than the Kapo who was taking over the morning routine, the counting time—the Appel. Afraid, we stood around in front of the barracks, surrounded by SS men. Some of them had dogs on leashes. It was frightening. The SS started to push us toward the middle of the camp, forcing us to run fast. The combination of the barking of the dogs and the voices of the SS hollering for us to move quickly made us feel that our end was near. This would be the last moment before they killed us. We were running. We did not have time to think. We had to move fast. I was pulling Chaim, pleading, "Let's stay together." At that moment I was telling my friend that this was the end, that the guards were going to kill us all. It took a while to get all of us in the center of the camp. The SS surrounded us and started to push, to squeeze us close together in one place.

We stood, afraid to move. I started to cry. At that moment I was reliving the liquidation of my ghetto in Radom, the selection of my loved ones to the Death Camp, as the SS with their dogs forced our people onto the cattle trains. The voices calling for help were ringing in my ears. I closed my eyes. A push from Chaim brought me back to the horrifying present. Chaim, trying to cheer me up, assured me this was not Radom. We stood and waited. I turned and saw a group of SS approaching, loudly calling for our Lagerelder (senior camp inmate). They left with him and returned a half hour later. The Kapos, following orders, began to organize prisoners into groups of one hundred, with a Kapo at the head of each column. This was something new for us. This was not the ordinary routine. The SS started to move in from the sides, surrounding each group. It was quiet. Only the voices of the SS shouting "Macht schnell" interrupted the silence.

We followed the orders without talking. It took an hour to completely form the columns. As we looked around, some of us raised our eyes to the sky, praying silently. We were standing, afraid to move, not knowing what was coming next. Seconds turned to minutes, the minutes turned to hours. So long was the wait—an eternity, waiting for the unknown. It was winter. A cold wind started to blow, Then, after awhile, it started to snow. The snow covered our tattered clothes. Then the sun came out and the snow started to melt. Under our feet the snow turned to water. When the sun went down the water turned to ice. Our wet clothes started to freeze and stick to our bodies. It was terrible. We had been standing in one place for so long. It was getting colder and colder. Those who could not take it any longer fell to the frozen ground, shaking from the cold. The Kapos started to hit them with their short sticks, trying to force them to stand up. Most of us had been standing, quietly, trying not to move. Only waiting and shivering. What else could we do?

Then a noise. From far away, we saw the Lager-fuehrer (camp commander) with a group of SS coming out of the office building with a paper in hand. He approached the Lagerelder, who was standing in the first group of one hundred. The Lagerfuehrer handed him a paper, turned around and returned to the office. The Lagerelder silently read the paper. When he finished he turned to talk to his helper. Then he moved quickly, going from one group to another, talking to the Kapos. Finally, we found out what was going on. We could breathe a little easier. Chaim turned to me and said, "Didn't I tell you that this is not Radom." I only shook my head. What else could I say? We had been lucky this time.

The orders required us to go back to our barracks and get our blankets. Also, we had to take our utensils with us, one spoon and one pot. We could take only one blanket with us. We were leaving the camp. This had to be done in a short time. We were given only twenty minutes to return from the barracks to be ready to move out. We ran as fast as possible, grabbing our blankets and utensils. We quickly returned to our groups. Breathing loudly, we stood in one place, waiting to move out. Chaim and I looked at each other. We both shook our heads and started to silently sob. I don't know why we cried. We were not allowed to talk. We did not have any other way to express our relief. There was so much tension. This was the only way to react. At least we knew what was going on. A Kapo stood at the front of each group of one hundred. The Lagerelder stood near the main gate, ready to move out. Chaim and I were in the first group of one hundred, ready to start our journey to the unknown.

Chapter Four

Pictures of My past

Before embarking on our trek, I ran back to the barracks, behind the latrines, where I dug out photographs I had buried when I first came to this camp. During the liquidation of our ghetto in 1942, my father ordered me to leave so that I could save myself. With tears in my eyes, I grabbed three pictures from our photograph album, and I ran from our home without looking back. These were the only tangible remains of my past, which I had carried from one death camp to another. These pictures were my steady companions; they have accompanied me in places where I experienced the deepest sorrow, and they were with me at the moment of my liberation, when I was rescued from Hell. They are still with me today.

I remember clutching the photographs in the cattle train as I arrived in Auschwitz and watched as Mengele sent my loved ones to the gas chambers. They were with me when I was in the hospital at Veihingen, where I hovered near death as a result of dysentery. I carried the pictures to the death camp at Schomberg where an SS man split open my skull. I made sure I had them when I was transported to my final camp at Spaichingen, where I hid them near the toilets. Now on this forced march I would take them, photographs of my sister Tania and my brother Isaac, neither of whom I had seen since 1942.

Joseph Freeman with his sister Tania and brother Isaac in 1938. He had this photo with him when he passed out before his liberation from the allies.

PART TWO

The Death March—
The Road to Hell

Chapter Five

The First Day on The Road

On the morning of March 16th the whistle blew and we started to move. Two of the SS men stood on either side of the main gate, counting the prisoners as they passed through. One group after another passed the gate. SS guards, some with dogs, were on either side of the columns. This was our escort. As we moved through the gate we saw three, maybe four horse carriages full of sick people who were surrounded by SS. We also saw some nurses with white jackets covering their striped uniforms. These were hospital personnel from our camp who were leaving with the sick as the hospital was evacuated. One hundred after one hundred passed through the gate going to the unknown.

It was already after midday. As we walked down the road, we looked back and saw our camp burning. The SS put our place of misery to the torch. We saw smoke rising high into the sky. From afar we could hear the sound of our camp buildings blowing up. This was the Nazi's tactic, not to leave behind any evidence of the atrocities that they had committed in that place. I was in the first column. As I looked ahead I saw a group of cars slowly moving ahead of us. Hungry and shaking from the cold, we moved along the road. Then we heard the sound of a whistle. The SS in front of us lifted his hand, signaling us to stop. A truck was waiting for us on the side of the road. Uniformed guards standing beside the vehicle gave us rations—a piece of bread and a cup of black watery solution that was supposed to be coffee. We were not allowed to stop. With the bread in one hand and the 'coffee' in the other, we were forced to keep on moving.

One thousand five hundred men, including the sick and the nurses, left Spaichingen. One thousand five hundred men started a journey on a road to Hell. At first we walked at a normal pace, but as time went by we slowed down. As we walked with our food in our hands, I turned to my friend and said, "Chaim, let's eat one piece of bread and share it together. The other piece we will eat this evening." He agreed. We ate only one piece and hid the other one. We were constantly moving along the icy road. One group after another passed the truck and received rations, then moved on. We walked for another two, maybe three hours. Soon a motorcycle with two soldiers drove by. One soldier was talking to the SS at the head of the column. When they finished talking the motorcycle drove away. After a while the SS blew a whistle and we stopped. He turned to talk to the Lagerelder, who then came back to our group to talk to the Kapo. The Kapo turned around and went from one group to another, talking to individual Kapos assigned to each column. It took a while. We stood and waited, wondering what was going on. When the Kapo returned to our group the Lagerelder lifted his arm. The SS in front blew his whistle and again we started to walk, moving from the road onto an open field.

We walked and it started to get dark. We came in front of three large barns. We stopped. The SS ordered the Kapos to divide us into three groups. My group went into the first barn, more than four hundred exhausted, hungry wretches. The rest were sent to the other barns. When we looked back we could no longer see the wagons carrying the sick prisoners. We did not know what happened to them. Tired and cold from an entire day on the road, we tried to find a place to lie down and rest. The barn, open on both sides, had only a roof and some supporting beams. I said quietly to Chaim, "Let's go inside. Let's try to get in the middle. It will be a little warmer than outside." We moved into the structure until we saw the roof over our heads. First, we put blankets on the frozen ground upon which we lay our cold, weary bodies. We then rolled ourselves into the blankets, leaving our heads out in the open, pushing our bodies close to each other. I reached into my pocket and pulled out the little piece of bread which we had been saving since morning. I divided it into two parts and gave half to Chaim. We ate it very slowly. After finishing it, we were still hungry. The wind started to blow. Shivering in the frosty night air, we could not sleep. The cold was starting to take over our bodies. It was so terrible; we were tired and hungry yet we could not fall asleep. We were afraid that if we closed our eyes we would freeze. We started to quietly sob. Tears were streaming down our cheeks. Some people next to us started to cry loudly. The Kapos tried to quiet them down, but the sobbing continued. So the Kapos started to hit them with their sticks. The crying stopped for awhile. When you are hungry, shaking from the cold, you slowly lose control of your emotions. You have to do something, and by making any kind of noise, you think this will help. Only those who went through Nazi hell will understand this moment of despair. You are not yourself. The cold has taken possession of your body. You are losing your mind. You feel you cannot function anymore. You aren't human anymore. This is the moment just before you are facing the end. Nothing matters anymore. We felt we had reached the end of the line.

Actually, this was just the beginning. Again, the silence did not last long. Some started to cry again. The Kapos, tired too, no longer paid attention to the moaning. We lay and just listened to the crying. After a while we forgot where we were. Some of us started to worship. The voices of the praying mingled with the sobbing and the voices calling for help, and the combination of these sounds made us feel very frightened. The SS, who had been watching us shot their guns into the air and shouted, "Schweigen schmutzige Jude" (Shut your mouths, you filthy Jews). Afraid to be killed, the voices quieted down. The night was so long. This was only our first night on the road. Sixteen hours had passed since we had been moved out of Spaichingen. We did not know what was in front of us; we were completely at the mercy of the devils, the SS.

Chapter Six

The Second Day on The Road

As the morning sun rose over the horizon, the doors to the barn were smashed open. The SS marched in, shouting at us to get up and move quickly. With their heavy boots they kicked those who were half asleep, forcing them to stand up. After a sleepless night on the frozen ground it was not easy to move. After one day on the march many of us were already showing signs of fatigue. As usual, the Kapos helped the SS force the inmates out into the open, forming them into groups of hundreds. The air of the winter morning was frigid. Shaking from cold and hunger, we moved, slowly. Some in our group fell down and we tried to lift them from the ground. They stood up, crying in anguish, and their tired bodies again dropped to the ground. The Kapos stepped in and hit these poor wretches with their short sticks. The cries of the people being hit mingled with the voices of Kapos trying to get them to move. Those of us who were able to stand were very depressed; still, those physically strong enough would continue to help those too weak to stand on their own.

There was neither the time nor the facilities to wash. Filth was starting to cover our faces and hands. We trudged along side roads as the SS tried to avoid populated areas. Someone viewing from a distance might have mistaken us for an entire military unit moving along the road. The column was led by the Lagerfuehrer in an open Mercedes Benz. That vehicle was followed by a few cars carrying the Lagerfuehrer's staff. Each unit of a hundred prisoners was headed by a Kapo, with an SS man ten feet in front. Other SS men guarded each side of the road, pointing their weapons in the direction of the prisoners. German shepherds accompanied some of the guards. The columns plodded forward, but many inmates began to slow down. We were hungry, thirsty, and filthy; the air around us grew heavy. Some in our group were unable to march in an orderly line. Those who straggled to the side were hit by irate SS men. Those who were not moving fast enough were set upon by vicious dogs who grabbed and bit their legs. Some of us tried to get the stragglers back into line, but there were too many straying all over the road. In addition, the Kapos attacked those of us trying to help our fellow prisoners. As the orderly line disintegrated, the Kapos ran around hitting people lying on the ground. The SS also beat those who could not keep pace. We constantly kept moving, afraid of being hit by the SS. Looking back, we saw that many prisoners had been pulled out of the line to the side. The SS surrounded them, pushing, prodding and hitting them in an effort to force them to move faster.

We had been on the road for many hours without a rest. I was holding on to Chaim, lumbering forward, pushing one foot in front of the other. The sun came out. As the day grew warmer, the blankets on our shoulders were getting heavy. But we held on to them, for they were the only protection from the night cold. Far ahead I saw an SS man on a motorcycle signaling for the column to stop. The SS moved us off the road to an open field. Two big trucks were waiting for us, one filled with bread cut into little pieces, and the other carrying a huge barrel of hot, steaming water. At first, we were happy to see the trucks since it meant we would receive our rations. But we had to form one orderly line and wait for further directions. It was terrible to feel the hunger pains with food so near, food which we could not touch without permission from our tormentors. Finally, the whistle blew and we moved toward the trucks. Someone broke ranks and the SS clubbed him. Afraid, we stood in line, patiently pushing our exhausted bodies forward to get our rations. Each of us received a small piece of bread and a cup of hot water. The guards did not permit us to stop, forcing us to eat while walking. We were afraid that we might spill our meager but precious portions which was our only source of nourishment. We had waited two hours to get our daily rations which we devoured in a matter of seconds. After I finished I felt more hungry than ever. Only those who have endured this hell can understand how we felt. We were helpless, at the mercy of the fiendish SS who were trying to starve us to death.

Chaim quickly swallowed his ration, placed his hands at his sides, and asked, "Is this all?" We were still hungry but the SS pushed us to move onto the road again. Fortunately, the pace was not as quick as the first day. There was not as many of us as there were yesterday. Missing were those the SS had ordered to walk at the end of the column. We did not know what happened to them.

We had been moving constantly on the road for several hours. Late in the day the weather grew cold, the wind began to blow a chill through us. Shortly afterwards, it began to snow. We pulled our blankets over our heads without stopping. About twenty minutes passed and the blankets were covered with snow. We had been so thirsty, we gathered the snow on the blankets and quickly swallowed it. After a few handfuls of snow got into my belly I felt terrible. I was doubled over with cramps. The pain was excruciating, bringing tears to my eyes. Others who had swallowed snow also fell ill. But we went on in pain, afraid to stop for fear of being beaten by the Kapos and the SS. Biting our lips in pain, we were forced to move on. I do not know how I had the strength to keep moving. It took awhile for the pain to diminish. I had learned my lesson—never swallow snow. I learned from this painful experience to put snow in my tin cup until it melted. Only then would I swallow it.

As the snow covered us, we became a line of white shadows pushing ahead. Every few minutes we had to shake the snow from our blankets because they were so heavy from the falling snow. It became difficult to move because the road was covered with snow and the footing was slippery. With each step the snow crunched under our boots. The snow was falling so heavily we could hardly see. People were coughing and sneezing. A whistle blew and we stopped. We were moved off the road onto an open field where we came to two large buildings. The SS divided us into two groups. Chaim and I were taken to the first building, along with many other prisoners. The room became very crowded and the SS slammed the door and locked it for the night. It was pitch dark and so packed with people that I could hardly move. Squeezed like sardines, holding on to Chaim in the dark, I looked for a place to sit. Turning our backs to each other, Chaim and I put one blanket on the frozen ground and sat on it, then wrapped the other blanket around us. There we sat, surrounded by a mountain of legs. The warmth of our bodies dissolved the ice on the ground, and the blankets we were sitting on started to get wet, whereas the blankets around our shoulders started to freeze. It was a frightening scene; sitting in the icy darkness, listening to the sounds of heavy breathing, coughing, and wheezing. The air quickly grew heavy, thick with the stench of the unwashed inmates pressed closed to each other. I felt as if I was closed inside a metal box. I started to choke from the foulness of the air. The frozen blanket at the back of my neck was cutting into my skin. I felt death nearby. I was biting my lip and slowly started praying to the Almighty that if this is the end, let it come quickly.

The pain I was feeling reminded me of when I was in a concentration camp at Schoemberg. I recalled the moment of my worst suffering when an SS man had cut the back of my neck with his knife. Covered with blood, I was dragged onto a pile of other victims either dead or writhing in agony. Lying among the casualties, I was covered with the excrements from the dead and the dying. In addition, the SS sprayed a solution getting us ready to be burned in a pit the following morning. The chemicals burned my eyes and left a bitter taste in my mouth. Then I heard the voice of my beloved Helen, calling, "Joseph, Joseph." While I was remembering this awful episode, I heard Helen's voice again.

Suddenly my head jerked back. The frozen blanket cut deep into my skin, the intense pain brought me back to reality. I was far away from Schoemberg, but very near my end. If I had not awoke from my stupor I would have frozen to death. The memories of Helen saved me. The combination of sweat and cold left my clothes glued to my body. The cold was literally taking over my body. I could only move my head. I spent another sleepless night, shaking from the cold. Suddenly the doors were swung open with great force. As the first light hit us, the SS ran into the room, screaming for us to get up. With the butt of their rifles they smashed those who moved too slowly. It was terrible. People running in panic, pushing and falling over one another in an effort to get out of the room and into the open. I will never forget the screaming and shrieking of those beaten by the murderous guards. I tried to get up but was knocked over by the impact of falling people. In the frozen shell of my clothing I managed to get up, helped by people around me. It was mayhem, inmates running wild, shoving indiscriminately. Somehow Chaim and I managed to get out of the building, to face another day of unbearable pain and suffering.

Chapter Seven

The Third Day on The Road

We stood in front of the building for some time until all the people were outside. As I looked around I saw so many who could barely move. "Macht schnell!" screamed the SS, but it was impossible to move quickly. We were cold, hungry, and the wet clothes were glued to our skin. As we began our third day on the road to Hell all I could see around me were desperate men trying to forestall the inevitable end. The faces of my fellow inmates had a ghastly quality: unshaven, covered with filth, and eyes red from lack of sleep. We looked like underfed animals wandering about in search of a final resting place.

As before, the SS, aided by the Kapos, organized us into groups of one hundred. At the start of our trek the SS had not behaved badly, but with each passing day they lost all sense of morality and they became cruel monsters. They seemed to enjoy inflicting pain on their helpless victims. We grew exhausted after hours on the road and we could not keep in an orderly line. We held on to each other, pushing our shivering, tired bodies forward. Those who fell down were set upon by the Kapos who beat them and forced them to move on. When the time came for our daily rations we were disappointed to see only one truck waiting for us. This time we received only a half a cup of cold water and a small piece of bread. The precious bit of food disappeared in seconds after which our appetites were stronger than ever. The little amount of water could not quench our thirst, and we grew progressively weaker.

Somehow we managed to push on until night fell. We left the road and came to a very large barn that was open on both sides. This was our resting place for the night. The SS pushed us inside and I grabbed Chaim by the hand, looking to settle in the middle of the building. We found a place to lay a blanket on the ground and we covered ourselves with the other blanket. It was cold and windy, but we were fortunate to be in the middle of the barn, surrounded by bodies on all sides. But the relentless hunger made it impossible to sleep. From the moment I closed my eyes I dreamed of FOOD, and plenty of it. In seconds I would awake to the terrible reality of starvation. It was impossible to move with more than one thousand pitiful souls squeezed under one roof. We were surrounded on all sides by the SS. They stood around some fireplaces outside the barn, smoking cigarettes and drinking.

For hours I lay on the ground with my eyes wide opened. I wondered, "Does my system work?" "Do I remember where I am?" I satisfied myself that I had not lost my mind, but I could not see any way out of my predicament. The nights were so long and the suffering was interminable. Every minute was an eternity of torment. It seemed as if morning would never come, and when it did, it meant facing another day of agony.

Chapter Eight

The Fourth Night On The Road

One day after another passed. We had been walking from morning until evening, resting at nights in open fields. The SS was constantly watching us. When we began the march we walked at a normal pace, but as the days passed, we slowed down. The SS pushed us, hollering for us to walk faster. Sometimes they hit us with their guns. At first the punishment succeeded in getting us to move quickly, but by the fourth day beatings could no longer speed the tempo of the walking. The people accepted the blows and still moved slowly. After awhile the SS stopped hitting us and they themselves started to slow down. Now some of us started to cough and sneeze. The cold was catching up to us. Some of us started to walk in groups of two, one supporting the other. Some began to fall on the ground. At first, one would pick up the other and support him while continuing to walk. But in time, the ones who could walk could not help those who had fallen. We were tired and also afraid of being hit by the SS.

Now we are coming to the most terrifying days of our journey. Come with me if you are psychologically and physically strong and can take it. You will understand how a human being turns into an animal, trying to survive in the most desperate moments when cold and hunger takes over his mind and body. "Dante's Hell" was a paradise compared to the living hell which I and my fellow survivors endured. We had been moving on the road for four days, trudging from morning until dark. Everyday, as we started to walk, we received our rations which consisted of a piece of bread and a cup of water. In the afternoon of the fourth day we moved out from the side road to the main highway. We saw German civilians, so many of them. Thousands and thousands were moving on the road, pushing handcarts full of personal belongings. Some were pushing wheelbarrows filled with household items. We also saw some wounded people in trucks moving in one direction. It was a parade without end, moving silently. Turning our heads, we saw them moving on the other side of the highway. The faces of the German civilians were tired and drawn. Some were in wagons sleeping or in a sitting position, shaking to the beat of the wagons moving on the bumpy roads. Some were moving on foot, including women carrying little children in their arms. It was a parade of human misery awash in a reign of terror and fright.

We had been moving constantly. The afternoon came, then evening. It started to get dark. A sound of the whistle and we stopped. We stood and waited. The SS in front of us talked to the Lagerelder. Another whistle and we started to move out from the highway to the side road. After walking for some time, we came to an open field. Some large empty buildings stood in front of us. Here we stopped for the night. I remember this very well, our fourth night of the march. It was the beginning of our inhuman suffering.

We were divided into two groups. Those of us in the first group entered the first building. As we entered we heard the shrill voices of the SS ordering us to move faster. We were frightened and cold. There were no wooden floors; we had to lay down on the frozen ground. Exhausted, hungry, and shaking from the cold, some of us could not take the hardship and started to cry and to pray. But praying could not help. Praying could not provide the warmth we desperately needed. The crying and the praying went on for the entire night. The night frost was the biggest killer. Each night some people gave up their will to live and died in their sleep. It was terrible after a long and painful night to awaken the next morning next to a friend, his face white, frozen, with pieces of ice jutting from the sides of his mouth. His tongue protruded like a piece of frozen red ice. He had given up. Others like him also gave up. They did not care anymore. There is a limit to pain and suffering. The breaking point comes and that little spark of hope is extinguished. This was the end of their pain. We did not know who was better off—they, the dead, or we who suffered but nevertheless went on. At first, the SS did not believe the inmates frozen on the ground were dead. They poked them with their guns. As this did not help, they shot into their dead bodies. We stood and looked as tears ran down our faces, silently watching the macabre scene. Some of us started to say Kaddish (the last prayers) in memory of our fallen comrades. We tried to get back to sleep but were awakened by Kapos kicking us and calling for us to get up. Laying for so long on the frozen ground, we were stiff and could hardly move. Then the SS who had been watching us from the outside of the building ran inside and started to hit us with the butts of their guns. Those still on the floor tried to escape the punishment by crawling around on the ground. But the SS were running after them and beating them. The sobbing from the victims and the excited voices of the SS barking orders mixed together and is still ringing in my ears. It was so long ago. Still I cannot forget the horrible scene of people crawling and the SS running after them and hitting them constantly.

We ran out from our miserable place of rest and looking back, we saw some inmates lying frozen on the ground. The SS ordered the Kapos to count them. We moved out, leaving some of our comrades unburied in the open. From now on death was out constant companion, reminding us that the end was closing in.

Chapter Nine

The Seventh Day on The Road

March 22nd, a full week since we were forced on the march. As far as the eyes can see there was a parade of miserable humanity moving silently on the road, moving without an end. We were surrounded on both sides by the SS. Snow covered the ditches on both sides of the highway. I turned to my friend, silently pointing out the snow with a shake of my head. He understood me. Quickly, Chaim and I bent down and grabbed handfuls of snow and put it quickly in our pants. It was done so fast that the SS did not notice it. I was so thirsty I had forgotten my earlier painful experience with swallowing snow. Each of us grabbed a handful of snow from our pockets, and tried to gobble it down out parched throats. My mouth was dry; I could not move my jaws. I had tears in my eyes trying to swallow the snow. I kept it in my mouth until it melted. Finally, as the snow turned to water, I pushed it down my throat and swallowed. It was very difficult. It was so painful. At last we had a few sucks of water. With the rest of the snow we wet our faces and hands. As we looked back we saw some of our group slowly bending down trying to pick up the snow. The SS caught them and started hitting them with the butts of their rifles, forcing them to throw away the snow which some were still holding in their hands.

The SS pushed some of the stragglers back into line. We had been slowing down. Some of us had to support others. We started to lean on one another, holding each other's arms. We started to move out from the line, going in groups of two and three. The SS did not care as long as we kept on moving. But as soon as someone stopped, the SS started to hit them and forced them to move on. There was no rest. The sun came out. It was getting a little warmer. The shirt on my back started to smell and became glued to my skin. We had been walking on the road for two, maybe three hours. Some of us could no longer walk. The SS stepped in, hitting us with the butts of their guns. Even still, some of us could not take another step. The SS turned the dogs on these helpless victims. The wailing of the inmates was terrifying as the dogs bit and ripped into their clothes and their flesh.

At first we tried to support one another. But we were too weak and tired and could no longer help the falling people. The crying of the people, the screaming voices of the SS, and the barking of the dogs filled us with despair. With so many injured and exhausted inmates lying on the road, it became difficult to move and we started to push one another. This angered the SS further, and they started to attack us. Suddenly, a miracle happened. Airplanes appeared on the horizon, flying toward us at an abnormal speed. The were coming closer and closer. Our marching column broke into a panic. People ran to the side of the road, pushing one another, making terrible noises, running for cover. The SS too fled from the road. I grabbed Chaim by the hand and we dove into some bushes at the side of the road. Everything was moving so fast. We lifted our heads and saw falling bombs ripping and cutting into pieces the group of cars at the head of our column. The noise of the exploding bombs was very scary. It was a terrifying scene, with mangled bodies littering the road. There were so many wounded crying for help.

The attack was over in seconds. The airplanes disappeared and left only destruction in their wake. We sat and watched, afraid to move. After a short time the SS returned. First, they inspected the wrecked cars at the front of the column. Then they inspected the remains of whatever was lying on the ground. They went to the side of the road, talking and arguing. We saw that the *Unterschutfuehrer* (non-commissioned officer) from our group was shouting orders. He was now in command, the highest ranking of the surviving SS. We stood and waited amid the dead and wounded lying on the road. Male nurses from our camp seemed to come from nowhere to move the wounded to the side of the road, and to pile corpses in another place. A group of SS left the road to search for anyone who had run away. Led by their dogs, the SS were running in all directions, looking for escapees. Then from far away, we heard shots. The SS captured some inmates who were immediately set upon by the dogs who ripped into their flesh. The SS pushed these bleeding prisoners and forced them to join our group. We now knew what would happen to us if we tried to escape.

We were again organized into groups of hundreds and we started to walk in formation, leaving our dead and wounded behind. We moved onto small side roads and walked until evening. This was the first time in our journey when so many people had been killed. The SS led us onto a large field with a storage building, open on both sides. This was our resting place for the night. It was impossible to understand how we could possibly go on, freezing at night, constantly hungry, unable to wash or change our clothes. Lice started to appear on our bodies. At first it didn't bother us, but as time passed the lice started to eat our flesh. I took off my shirt and cleaned off the insects but after awhile I didn't care anymore. The hunger and cold was inflicting more pain than the insects. I got used to them. But the cold and especially the hunger was so bad that I thought I was going crazy. Our stomachs became swollen after a week of drinking snow from the side of the road. As we lay on the frozen ground at night trying to sleep, we got cramps and our stomachs made strange gurgling noises. I bit my lip from pain and I was constantly shivering and crying.

The morning following the air raid I could not find our Lagerelder. He had fled during the confusion of the attack. From now on the SS took over our group, or what was left of us. The Kapos were no longer in charge; now the SS would shout orders directly at us. We had to obey them quickly. But these masters of our destiny were, too, losing their resolve. At times we saw some of them take off, disappearing from the side of the road. At other times, we were joined by new groups of prisoners.

Chapter Ten

One Month Into The March

E ver hungry and shaking from the cold, we continued to trudge along the highway. When the Unterscharfuehrer took over command of our group, things got worse for us. We didn't get rations on a daily basis. The little food we received was barely enough to keep us alive. The SS was trying to starve us to death. Every other day we would get a small piece of bread and a cup of cold water. No more hot water. After a sleepless night in the open, we waited to receive this little morsel of bread and a few precious sips of water. Some mornings we were disappointed; we waited for our rations but instead the SS forced us to move out onto the main road.

Tired and shivering, we could hardly move but we had to. Again, so many of us could not make it anymore. We left many stiff bodies, frozen in the place of our night's rest. The SS did not care any longer. They rushed us out. No time to look back. We dragged ourselves out on the road for another day of misery. We had been moving slowly, the same routine, one foot in front of the other. We pushed our bodies forward, one supporting another. No more walking in groups of hundreds.

The Kapos walked with us, no longer at the head of the group. The SS took over and pushed us to move along. The hitting lost its effect. People got used to being beaten. The SS hit the fallen prisoners. When this did not help they killed them and pushed their bodies into ditches on the side of the road. We did not care anymore. We had been walking half asleep. I was holding onto Chaim and he was holding onto me. We found a way to sleep and walk at the same time. I would close my eyes for a few minutes, slowly pushing my body forward, then Chaim would close his eyes while walking for a few minutes. It was a parade of moving shadows. Thirsty, our lips began to crack. My tongue was so dry I felt I was choking. It became impossible to swallow. We were moving and sobbing, afraid to stop. Death was now following us. So many of us had been killed by the SS. For them, this was routine. Time was moving so slowly. When you suffer, every second is long.

Another day was coming to an end. It was getting dark. Again the SS ordered us off the main road. Again there was an open field. As I looked back I saw our group was getting smaller. Exhausted and famished, we could barely move. We crawled to the front of a large building. The SS ordered us in. I grabbed a few handfuls of grass and quickly put it in my pocket. Chaim had the opportunity to grab a few pieces of ice from the frozen ground. Once inside, we covered ourselves with blankets. I pulled out a few blades of grass and mixed it with the melted snow. We swallowed this strange mixture, but still our hunger kept us awake. The night, so miserable and terrible, lasted forever. Insects were eating their way into our clothing, but the cold and hunger were worse than the bugs. We were constantly coughing and sneezing. Unshaven, disheveled from the same clothes we had been wearing for weeks, we began to look like monsters. Gradually, we began to behave like animals, hopeless beasts at the mercy of butchers, waiting to be slaughtered without emotion.

The nights were the worst. We were dying of hunger, yet for the SS who watched us there was plenty of food to eat. We watched them eat, which only made us more aware of our hunger. The SS stood around their warm fireplace and gazed upon us as we lay on the frozen ground, shaking and shivering from the cold. The guards were enjoying their cigarettes, eating and drinking vodka. This was unbearable for us; we were no longer human.

One particular moment will always stay with me, an episode which shows what hunger can do to a so-called human body. It was the night after a very long and painful day early in April. As always, the SS were standing around the fireplace, eating their rations. One officer became sick and went to the side of the road. He doubled over and began to vomit. Chaim and I had been lying on the ground, not too far from the fire. Chaim quietly whispered that he was going to go and pick up the food the soldier had just thrown up. I admonished him, "You cannot eat that. It is sour." He turned to me and said, "I'm hungry. This is food." He crawled over to where the soldier had thrown up and swallowed the vomit left on the ground. Chaim came back and after a while, he threw up too. Others had been watching what was going on. At the moment Chaim began to vomit, a few of the starving people, like wild animals, threw themselves on the liquid remains, devouring it in seconds. This is what hunger can do. You appear human, but you are not any longer. Hunger can transform you into something less than human. It was so terrifying to witness this. The SS had turned us into monsters and this was in April 1945, a few weeks before liberation. Not many of us lived to tell about the last moment of the living hell we suffered.

More than one thousand five hundred inmates, counting the sick started on the death march. The nurses told me that on the first evening the SS separated the casualties from the main group. They were ordered to take the sick and wounded down from the carriages and put them in one place. As the nurses left the area they heard machine guns and the screams of the slaughtered. When the march began I could not see the end of our procession. Now, after four weeks on the road, I could see the end of the column which had been getting shorter each day. Two hundred or maybe four hundred emaciated wretches were crawling on the road. We looked hideous, our unshaven faces covered with filth, our hair breeding grounds for lice. The stench from our unwashed bodies was indescribable. The stinking odor was overwhelming, making it almost impossible for us to breathe.

In a single day we would walk three, maybe four miles. At times we passed small villages, where townspeople gazed at us from the sidewalks. As we passed through one small town, apples began to rain upon us. Never will I forget that moment. Like animals, we fell on one another, grabbing apples and devouring them in seconds. The SS responded by smashing us with the butt ends of their weapons. But the drive to satisfy our hunger was stronger than the punishment inflicted by the officers. Residents on both sides of the street were horrified and started to cry. These German civilians could not bear to witness this harrowing, dreadful scene. They too knew despair. They could not stand to watch the misery of living skeletons fighting to catch something to eat. These burghers could still feel human compassion, unlike the SS who were "Satans" in human form.

We marched through other towns where people tried to help us by throwing pieces of food toward us. Not all German civilians could feel the suffering of other human beings. In some places the residents were openly hostile to us. They laughed at us when the SS prevented us from catching the little morsels of apple or bread. They teased us and cursed us, calling us *schmutzige Hunde* (filthy dogs). Maybe because they had been indoctrinated with the philosophy of the super race, they could no longer feel compassion for the pain and suffering of others. These were the future leaders of the so-called "Nazi Empire." It is hard to understand how people can change so quickly from builders to destroyers. This was the reality of the Nazi Weltanschauung philosophy, a paradise built on the misery of so-called *Untermenschen*, the lower class of humanity. We did not think about these things at the time of our suffering. We were dying of hunger and sickness; there was no time to ponder. But now, so many years later, looking back, I can understand why the majority of Germans failed to face the challenge. They took the easy way out, forsaking any code of ethics and morality toward their fellow humans.

In the weeks and days before the "Thousand Year Reich" was collapsing, we prisoners continued to agonize and to perish. As spring approached, the days grew warmer. We were barely surviving on a diet of grass, leaves and melted snow. I was dying piece by piece. The suffering of my fellow inmates was my suffering. I was not myself any longer. I was a part of a body of a hundred men, a collective body that was slowly expiring. Part of me was still living, but as inmates were dying with every passing hour, a part of me was dying too. It was a slow death. In a moment one can see the Angel of Death. This is the end. Humans die only once. I'm not human. I died a thousand times and I came back to life. Death was not an end to my suffering; I was death alive. There was no end to my agony.

In the last weeks of the death march we met a group of SS men escorting other inmates. We had no idea of where they came from. The SS from our group were engaged in an animated conversation with the SS escorting the other group. Then, after a while, the new group joined our column. As the two groups merged, we saw three trucks on the side of the road loaded with sacks of food. This was the price they had to pay to join our group. The SS from our group had made a good deal. They received a lot of food in exchange for a handful of new inmates to oversee. These new prisoners would be dead in a few days anyway. It looked as though the new group had been on the road for a long time. The new SS wore heavy, warm clothes: snowboots, fur coats, and raincoats with head covers. But their charges were poorly dressed and had no covers for their heads. Their faces were yellow. True, we looked repulsive, but the newcomers did not look any better, the only difference being they did not smell as bad as we did.

That night the same scene repeated itself. We rested on frozen ground in an open field, surrounded by the well-fed SS. The smoke from their cigarettes and the smell of the vodka and pieces of salami drove some of the starving inmates crazy. Some could not take it anymore. They started to run and the SS sent the dogs after them. In just a few minutes we could hear the cries of the runaway prisoners. The barking of the dogs and the shouting of the SS still ring in my ears. Shots rang out and then the silence. The SS returned with the dogs, who were covered with blood. Some of us quietly said Kaddish for those who had been killed. We could not sleep. I did not know how much longer we could go on.

The end was approaching for the last surviving inmates from Spaichingen. People were dying every day and night. The new SS men behaved more brutally than the former ones. If an inmate could not walk or fell down, he was immediately pulled from the line and shot. I felt I had reached my end. The pain and the inhumane conditions were catching up with me. I had lost so much weight I was reduced to skin and bones. When I received my ration it was very hard for me to reach my hand to my mouth to eat the little piece of bread. My hands were shaking uncontrollably. Inmates were lying and rolling on the ground with blood oozing from their mouths. The SS shot those who were laying down. This living Hell was an eternity.

A day after the new group joined us, the Unterscharfuehrer changed the routine. We rested during the day and marched in the evening. It appeared to me that we were avoiding villages and cities. Only one hundred and fifty inmates from Spaichingen Death Camp remained alive. During the four weeks of our forced march the SS had killed more than one thousand three hundred people.

Chapter Eleven

A Face From The Past: The Story of Leo Goldfarb

A few days had passed. Other inmates joined our column, survivors from another camp. There were only twenty prisoners in the group, but there was also a large contingent of additional SS. The newcomers were in very bad shape. They were walking skeletons, poorly dressed with boots that were falling apart. I thought I recognized a face from the new group. I turned to Chaim and said, "Chaim, if I'm not mistaken, I saw a face from the city of Radom, my hometown." "Forget it, you are dreaming," he said. I approached the group and turned to the man and asked, "Aren't you from the city of Radom? Is your name Liebel Goldfarb?" "Yes," he responded. I asked him to join me and my friend. It was hard for him to stand up. Looking at him struggle, I saw what terrible shape he was in. His legs were swollen like wooden posts. His shoes were cut on the side. They were too small for him so he ripped them open so that his feet could fit into them. His pants were open at the front and were too small for him. They were tied with a rope. His face was bloated, his eyes were dark. I remembered that this man had been one of the wealthiest people in the city of Radom. Shortly before the war he had married the daughter of the most respected family in our city, the family Den. Her name was Feigusia. She was a friend of my mother's sister, Lea. At the time of the war this man gave a lot of money to the Jewish community in our city, money which had been used to buy food and clothing for the poor. I had been to his house when I was working in the disinfection department in our ghetto. He gave me one hundred zlotys (equal to one hundred dollars). I remember it very well. Now, looking at this shadow of a man, tears filled my eyes. He slowly began to tell what had happened to him.

Two months earlier, when the Russian army was nearby, the SS evacuated their camp. Eight hundred prisoners were forced to march day and night, without rest. In one week more than five hundred had been killed. After ten days on the road, the SS slowed down. Almost all the marchers were sick. The inmates had been getting by each day on just a little piece of bread and some water. The small group of twenty inmates who joined us was all that remained of the eight hundred on the forced march. Chaim and I looked at each other and shook our heads.

Evening came and it was time to move on. We got our ration of a small piece of bread and water.

We helped our new friend to get up. We held him from both sides and began walking on the road. We moved very slowly. After an hour it was getting hard for us to continue. We turned to Leo and told him we could not help him anymore. He asked us to leave him by the side of the road. With our last strength from our dying bodies, we dragged him to the side of the road and gently laid him down. Chaim and I were crying as we left him there. We then pushed our weary bodies to continue the journey.

After a few minutes shots rang out. I squeezed Chaim's hand. With tears in our eyes we looked up to the sky and said the first verse of Kaddish in memory of the fallen victims murdered by the SS. We asked some officers what they did with those who were put on the side of the road. They said in German, *"Wir haben dem umgelegt"* (We killed all of them). So one more of our people joined the ones who had been killed on Kiddush Hashem. We saw that the end was coming for us.

Chapter Twelve

Jacob, The Young Martyr

We lost track of time. Each day was like the day before. But we did notice that the days were growing warmer, that spring was on the way. Little flowers and grass started to appear in some places. Mother Nature was bringing rejuvenation, but for us there was only continued agony and torment. The road was littered with our deceased companions, each corpse a testimony to inhumane cruelty. It seemed impossible to go on, yet there we were, human skeletons pushing our exhausted bodies along the road. Weary, starving, and shaking from the cold, each moment felt like it would be our last. But we moved on, pushing forward in pain, afraid to stop. Days and nights passed with the same routine; our suffering was without end.

The worst was waiting to get our rations. It was the only thing we could look forward to, but sometimes we did not get it. It is impossible to describe the disappointment. When you are starving your entire system aches for even the smallest bite of bread and a few spoonfuls of water. Such meager morsels were the key to survival and being denied that little bit of food became too much for some. I saw inmates drop to the half frozen ground, kicking their legs in the air. White mucous frothed from their mouths. They cried and made loud, anguished screams. then, in a matter of seconds, they stopped. Silence. Death relieved them of their suffering. I looked upon this macabre scene without emotion. The feeling of being human had died within me; hunger and misery had possessed me. My mind did not work right. My fellow prisoners and I stepped over the bodies of our fallen comrades, our eyes wide open, like a herd of sheep waiting its turn for the slaughter. We were the living dead.

Yet we still clung to the thin thread of life. We tried to find something to eat. Leaves from trees, grass from the side of the road—we reached for anything that appeared edible. The SS no longer tried to stop us; they knew that we would soon be dead. It is very difficult to relive this time of unfathomable desperation. The experience of starvation left an indelible scar on my psyche; it was so long ago, but the grief and misery of those days touched me to my core and will stay with me as long as I go on living.

Every day our column grew progressively shorter but at times new groups would join us, accompanied by more soldiers and SS men. The new arrivals were in terrible condition, but the SS were clad in warm clothes and heavy boots. I remember one contingent of inmates in particular, their faces swollen, their clothes in tatters. Many of them had rugs wrapped around their legs. After a night on the road, we were resting in an open field. We sat not too far from these unfortunate souls. Slowly, I approached them and started to talk. At first I spoke in German. No response. Then in Polish. Then Yiddish. Only one of them answered. His name was Jacob, a lad of nineteen. I found out that he and his compatriots were survivors from Auschwitz. Their story of starvation and suffering was similar to ours. Like us, they were constantly on the march, constantly subjected to the brutality and ruthlessness of the SS. Jacob Gutman, my companion in misery, shared his story.

When World War II broke out he had been living with his family in a small village not far from Kielce, a city some 80 miles south of Warsaw. His family had been farmers for generations and had managed to live with their Polish neighbors without serious disturbances. But when the Germans invaded in September, 1939, many Poles began to turn against Jews. Jacob stopped for awhile, recalling the painful moments of his past. Then he continued with his account. The SS came to his house accompanied by several Polish people who had been identifying Jewish people for their German masters. Some of the Polish collaborators were his neighbors. The SS gave him and his family twenty minutes to leave. He was terrified seeing his parents grabbing their belongings, crying. Everything had to be done in a rush as the German officers hollered at them to move more quickly. As soon as they left their house, the Poles rushed inside to remove the furniture. Jacob was now breathing loudly, tears streaming down his face. "My father tried to get back into the house," he reported. "One of the SS men started to hit him. My father turned around and pushed the soldier away. In a split second, the SS man pulled out his revolver and shot. My father fell to the ground. My mother ran to protect my father. The SS man turned toward her and with one shot to the head killed my mother." He stopped, covering his face, sobbing uncontrollably.

I looked at him and started to cry. I, too, was reliving the past, when the SS man hit my mother, pushing her toward the cattle wagons that carried her and my sister to the death camps. Blood covered my mother's lovely face. She called out for help but there was nothing I could do. I shared with Jacob my moment of horror and humiliation. Chaim too was sitting silently, listening to both of us. The three of us realized we had been through the same hell.

Jacob told us he had been on the road for nearly four months. The SS had evacuated his camp at night with the Russian army closing in. More than four thousand inmates began wandering from one place to another. They started in winter and by the time they joined us, fewer than one hundred had survived. Suddenly, Jacob cried out that he could not move his legs.

He asked me to help him. I peeled back the rugs covering his legs and felt they were wet with blood. Chaim and I moved Jacob to a comfortable position. I held my breath as I looked at his wounds. Both of his legs were badly infected. His right leg was swollen and the skin had turned dark blue. In some places the flesh was opened and covered with dried blood, while fresh blood oozed from other sores. He could not move his toes, which were bloated. I ripped part of my blanket into long pieces, which served as bandages for his mangled legs. I had learned how to do this when I worked at a death camp hospital in Schoemberg. But I knew that if he did not get immediate treatment, he would die from his infections. I prayed to the Almighty. "God, where are you? Please help me. This boy is so young, why does he have to die? Hasn't he suffered enough?" I was afraid I would break down. What could I do to help him? I didn't have water to wash his wounds, I had no medicine to administer. I talked softly to Jacob, trying to calm him down. I was sweating as I wrapped the swathes of blanket around his swollen legs. That was all I could do. He needed help and he needed it quickly. Chaim and I did the best we could to make him feel comfortable. We put a blanket behind his head and told him to rest, and that we would be getting our daily rations in a few hours. Jacob closed his eyes and fell asleep. Chaim and I sat by him in silence. We looked at each other, just shaking our heads. After awhile we fell asleep only to be abruptly woken by the hysterical shouts of the SS, ordering us to get up. I nudged Jacob but he did not move. Weeping, I told Chaim, "Jacob is dead." I looked at the young face and raised my eyes to the sky, crying, "Lord, how long do we have to suffer? Is this not enough? Please help us, wherever you are. Put an end to our suffering." The SS pushed us to move out. I took a last look at Jacob, saying Kaddish, the prayer for the deceased. We moved out onto the road, leaving behind the remains of Jacob and many others who had died while we rested in the open field. Yet another soul had departed this living hell.

Chapter Thirteen

Blood Alley

It was sometime in the middle of April. The monotonous routine continued, resting during the day and marching at night. We began to look like wild creatures, our faced dirtied and covered with hairs, our eyes wide-opened and set back. Our clothes were glued to our skin, infested with flesh-eating insects. But the pain and the hunger were worse than these parasites, and we got used to them. Besides, we were too weak to take the shirts off our backs.

Something, however, was different. We began to realize that many of the SS guards who had begun the march had run away; only the *Untersharfuehrer* (non-commissioned officer) and his two helpers remained from the original detachment. We were now guarded by other SS who had joined us on the road. These new oppressors were worse than those they replaced. They were more cruel and sadistic, playing a cat and mouse game with us. Previously, the SS would take those who could not keep up to the side of the road. Only after the column moved out of sight would they shoot the victim. Now however, the new guards did not wait to kill stragglers. The moment someone slowed down or fell, these monsters would command specially-trained German shepherds to attack. The dogs grabbed the fallen inmates by the legs. With razor-like teeth they ripped out pieces of flesh. The agonizing screams from the victims made the dogs even more aggressive. But this was only the beginning of the torture. As the wounded prisoners lie on the ground, the SS called off the dogs and they took over, smashing the crying inmates with the butts of their guns, shouting, *"Aufstehen schmutzige Jude!"* ("Get up, dirty Jew!"). The blood spurting from open wounds did not deter the SS from their murderous work. The cries of the tortured still ring in my ears. I can never erase that moment of pain and inhumanity. Once the crying stopped, the SS finished off the victim with a gunshot to the head. Pools of blood spread around the bodies lying on the road.

The guards forced us to watch the atrocity and warned us that this would be our fate if we stumbled on the march. We stood silent, biting our lips. We did not react; in shock, we were incapable of crying—the pain, the terror, and the hunger having robbed us of much of our human emotion. The road was covered with blood, evidence of the monstrous brutality of the SS.

We were convinced the end was near, that none of us would survive. Worse, most of us were transformed into unfeeling robots who no longer cared whether we lived or died. However, a handful of us miraculously retained the will and the hope of survival. But that spark was dying as we passed the bodies of friends lying on the road. I held onto Chaim, silently saying Kaddish for our murdered companions.

Chapter Fourteen

Five Minutes Before Twelve

April 25th, 1945. We had been on the road for so many days, so many weeks. I lost track of time. I could not remember anymore. My mind had stopped working. I could not count anymore. The hunger and the cold had taken over. I was no longer human. We had been walking night after night. So many of us had been killed by the SS. The road was littered with dead bodies. The SS did not care anymore. They just left the dead on the road and forced us to walk. They forced us to move fast, but we could not. The beatings had no effect. We mostly just pushed our tired bodies one leg in front of the other. It was so painful to walk. We walked many hours each night. Every movement was torture. I was mostly being supported by my friend Chaim, who constantly reminded me not to stop. He would say, "Joe, you saw what the SS have been doing. The moment you are on the ground the SS will kill you. You have to walk. Another hour and we will stop for a rest. Please don't give in." With tears in his eyes, he begged me to go on. He was my friend, the only one at that moment, when death was the master of our destiny. Crying, I pushed my body forward, slowly, one foot in front of the other.

We began to realize that some of the SS had been disappearing. This only happened at night, on the road. The SS took the sick away to be killed, and they did not return. They disappeared. The new SS who joined our columns were often worse than those they replaced. It looked as if they had come from Russian territory once occupied by the Nazis, retreating as they evacuated and took death camp inmates with them. They unloaded the bitterness of defeat on the dying inmates, sadistically killing sick and helpless victims. We had been observing how these "heroes" behaved in the last days before liberation. At the moment we saw planes on the horizon these officers of the "master race" ran away, afraid of being caught, shedding their uniforms in an attempt to save their skins. We stayed, afraid to move. We did not have enough strength to run away.

After what seemed like forever, the SS ordered us to lay down by the side of the road. No more going onto open ground. We had been falling down, helplessly holding onto each other. It was getting lighter. I was lying on the side of the road, crying silently. I put my hand into my shoe and when I withdrew I saw that it was covered with blood. I told Chaim, "I cannot wear my shoes anymore. They are cutting deep into my feet which are starting to bleed." I asked my friend to help me take my shoes off my feet. He cut my blanket into pieces which I wrapped around my feet. I felt relief for awhile. Still I was lying on the ground and could not sleep. I was hungry and sick, and I could not see very well. I saw dark fragments flying before my eyes. I forgot where I was. My mind did not work anymore. I was so hungry. My head was burning. I started to sweat and cry from hunger. Chaim tried to calm me down. He put his hand over my mouth, gently cautioning, "Remember, be quiet, otherwise the SS will kill you." With tears streaming down my face, I began choking and sobbing. How terrible it was, exhausted and starving and unable to sleep because the cold took over my body. Added to this, the noise in my stomach from the hunger constantly reminded me that I was still alive. Painfully, I lay there and pressed my stomach to quiet the noise, but this did not help. My friend was again trying to comfort me, telling me, "Hold on. Soon we will get a piece of bread and some water." I was laying there crying silently, hungry and tired, turning from side to side, until I finally fell asleep; for how long I do not know. Suddenly I felt Chaim pushing me, trying to wake me. I opened my eyes and started to cry. Hungry, half frozen from the cold, my friend was trying to lift me from the ground. "Come on, we have to move. Time to go." I shook my head; it did not seem possible to go further. After struggling to my feet I saw that I could walk. I had no shoes, just rags on my feet. The SS did not care, just as long as I moved. I lifted my body, or what was left of it. As I walked my joints ached, but I knew if I stopped moving it would be the end of me.

Chaim was holding onto me and I to him. We made it to the road and pushed our bodies forward, slowly and painfully. We were at the head of the column. When we started our journey it was impossible to see the end of our column as we looked back. Now, as we looked back, we could see that there were no more than one hundred living corpses straggling down the road. That was all who remained to bear witness to the horror, the ones who had miraculously gone through hell and somehow survived.

After several hours of struggling to stay on my feet, feet covered with nothing but a few rags, I turned to Chaim and said, "I can't walk anymore." Supporting me with his arms, he pleaded, "Joe, you have to go on." he was pulling me, pushing me, forcing me to walk. It was becoming impossible for me to move my legs. He pulled me for another ten minutes, but I did not have the strength to move. I could only see black in front of my eyes. I remember my last words to Chaim, "You go on, my friend, I cannot take it anymore. What will be, will be. You go on. You can't help me. This is the end for me." Still, he was trying to lift me, but my body was too heavy for him. I was gesturing for him to leave me. Crying, with the last strength left in my body, I pushed him away from me. He gently folded my blanket and covered me with it. Then, still looking at me, he waved with his hand a farewell. Crying, he went back to the road.

I was lying on the side of the road, shivering with cold and hunger. Sick. I could not see anymore. Everything was getting dark. I was so hungry. My mind didn't work any longer. I closed my eyes, trying to sleep. I tried to still my empty stomach that was making strange gurgling noises. I moved from one side to the other until I finally fell asleep. But not for long. I awoke, afraid. It was night, the moon was shining. I lifted my head and looked toward the road where I saw many people walking slowly, silently. So many moving on the road, without a sound. Some of them held little children in their arms. The line of refugees moved without end.

It was a parade of shadows moving on the highway. I saw horse-drawn wagons filled with people. They did not look at me as they passed by. It was hard for me to lift my head. Shivering from the cold, I put my hand into my pocket and took out the picture of my brother and sister, which I had carried with me since the beginning of the war. With shaking hands I gazed at it and started to cry, silently. Then, with my last strain of energy, I raised my voice to call out, "Lord, how long? Is this not enough? I can't take anymore. Haven't I suffered enough? Please help me. Take my life. Put an end to my pain. This is the end of me. I'm so hungry and so sick. Why must I suffer so much? I'm only flesh and bones. I'm going crazy. Please make an end of my suffering." I held the picture in my hand, kissed it, and with my eyes closed I quietly prayed, *"Sh'ma Yisrael Adonai Elohaynu Adonai Echad."* I felt tears running down my face. Then I passed out, for how long I do not remember.

PART THREE

Deliverance

Chapter Fifteen

The First Days of Liberation

It was still night and I was lying on the road. I could not sleep. I had terrible pains in my legs; I could not move them. I felt as though I was losing control of my mind. My head was on fire, I could hardly see. My hands started to shake. I was so hungry. I was reaching out, trying to catch some of the snow which was falling around me. I caught some and wet my head and face. I felt a little better. I looked up and saw the moon brightening the darkness. With my last bit of strength I lifted my head and looked out on the road. A column of people was moving constantly, silently, slowly—a parade of shadows, moving without end. So many of them, these moving phantoms, pushing little handcarts filled with personal belongings. Some were civilians, others were soldiers, unarmed and wounded, just shuffling forward in a straight line. The darkness was giving way to the first light of dawn. The first rays of the sun started to brighten the sky. It was the beginning of another day, but my pain did not stop.

Time did not stop. I was suffering and dying. Could this be my last day on Earth? The sky darkened, then streaks of light came from far away, followed by thunder. The lightning and thunder seemed to come closer and closer in my direction. The people on the road started to move faster, pushing one another, making noises, running to the side of the main road. Barely able to lift my head, I saw soldiers and heard the noises of tanks rolling down the road—afraid and shaking, I passed out. I do not know how long I was unconscious, but when I awakened the first thing I saw when I opened my eyes was a face full of sweat. The soldier who was bending over me called to his friends, "Hey, here is one more still alive." His voice still rings in my ears. I was scared and I made a noise. He talked to me in a very gentle tone and tried to quiet me down. He washed the filth from my face and poured water into my mouth. I started to cough and choke. He began to talk to me, very gently, trying to comfort me, but I could not understand what he was saying. I could only look at him and cry. This was the first hand that had reached out to me, not to hit me, but to help me. This was the hand of an American G.I. This was the moment of my liberation, the end of my suffering. The Angel of Death was reaching out to get me and then seconds later, a young soldier brought me back to life.

Never, as long as I live on this Mother Earth, will I ever forget that moment. More soldiers came by and spread a blanket on the back of a jeep. They lifted me from the ground and gently placed me on the blanket, covering and comforting me. I was still shaking from the cold and crying, but this time I was crying for joy. After so many years of pain and suffering, I had forgotten how to smile. With tears in my eyes, I could not speak, I could only look at them—my liberators. I could not understand what had happened to me. It had happened so quickly. It was very difficult for me to comprehend reality—from death to life in a matter of seconds! Impossible.

The soldiers placed a piece of chocolate in my hand. I had not seen chocolate in so many years. I was afraid to eat it. I was crying and laughing at the same time. The soldiers around me could not fathom my behavior. I came from another universe, a planet called Auschwitz, an alien world with a logic and way of life impossible for any civilized person to comprehend. The soldiers could not understand me as I emerged from the shadow of death. This was the moment I prayed for and dreamed about. But when the moment finally came, it was very hard for me to readjust. No more beatings. No more humiliations. I felt like a frightened dog constantly punished by his master, I was afraid to move. For the previous four years I had the mind of a slave, head bowed, obeying orders from tyrants whose cruelty was beyond imagination. My mind, in the first moments of liberation, did not work right. I was half dead, sick, dying from starvation. Then suddenly, without notice, everything changed so drastically. I was fortunate that I did not go crazy. How could someone who had not experienced such trauma possibly understand my reaction? Furthermore, I could not understand what the GIs were talking about since I knew not a word of English. But the way the soldiers took care of me made me feel so good. Then an American Chaplain drove by in a jeep and spoke to me in German, "Du bist frei" (you are free). His words were sweet, confirming that my suffering had come to an end. I had survived. So many thousands of innocent people had been slaughtered by the SS; up to the very end the SS had been killing my friends. The cruelty was beyond comprehension, beyond imagination.

I was liberated about one kilometer from Fussen, a city in southern Germany near Bayern. I was taken by jeep to a hospital. Relive with me as I stepped from death to a normal way of life. My clothes, filthy and covered with lice, were taken from me. Then a shower. With a brush the hospital attendants removed the filth from my body. After that, they shaved me all around. They then put me in a bath tub, my first bath in four years! When they finished cleaning me I climbed out of the tub and looked in a mirror. I saw the image of a stranger who was nothing more than skin and bones. I could hardly stand. Nurses held me by both arms and helped me to walk. Gently, they tried to place me on a bed covered with clean sheets. Holding onto the edge of the bed with both hands, I began to sob out loud. I had not seen a bed for so many years, I could not remember when I had seen such clean sheets. I was crying uncontrollably and the nurses around me started to cry.

I realized that the transition from death's doorstep to a normal way of life was not going to be easy. I was still living in the shadow of death. I could not believe I was free.

The nurses slowly put me on the bed. I was still crying, just shaking my head and touching the sheets. I still did not believe what was happening to me after all I had been through. They brought me food on a tray. I looked at the nurses and fingered the food, not eating, only crying. Just a few hours earlier I was dying from hunger and here I was with food in front of me. It was too unbelievable! Instead of celebrating my first day of freedom I was living in yesterday, in the days of hell. The pain was still fresh, I needed time to forget. Everything was moving too fast. I was too weak, physically and mentally, to cope with it. I needed time. I was afraid I would go crazy. It was too much for me. The nurses tried to help me to eat. I was tired, I closed my eyes and put my head down. The nurses gently put my head on the pillow. Breathing hard, I soon fell asleep. They turned off the lights and left the room.

I don't know what happened to me. I awakened and I forgot where I was. The room was dark. I started to cry, hitting the wall with my fists. The nurses came running in, trying to comfort me, explaining to me where I was and not to be afraid. I was frightened by the darkness. From the moment I closed my eyes, I was back on the road to hell. The anguished cries of people being killed by the SS rang in my ears. I saw the faces of my loved ones who were stretching out their hands as the SS beat them and pushed them into the cattle cars. I saw the sadistic look on the faces of the SS as they witnessed little children thrown out of windows from second and third floor stories. The SS stood in front of the buildings, some would shoot at the little ones as they plummeted to their death. I could not erase the image of one officer with a bottle of vodka in one hand and a revolver in the other, laughing and clearly enjoying himself. I was standing in horror with my family as we looked at this macabre spectacle. I recalled my mother turning to my youngest sister Tania, covering Tania's eyes trying to spare her from seeing the brutality of the SS. My mother then looked at me, crying, shaking her head in disbelief. That was 1942 at the liquidation of our ghetto in Radom, Poland. Without words my mother tried to say, "What else can I do to protect her?" This was my mother, trying to protect us as best she could in an impossible situation.

I was free but I was suffering. I went through so much pain and the memories were too raw to forget. For much of that first night I just sat and wept. I quieted down after awhile but I could not go back to sleep. I sat on the bed, gazing out the window. My first night of freedom was filled with recollections of yesterdays so filled with tragedy for me, my family and my people.

When I arose from bed in the morning, again I relived my personal hell. I remembered how I was exposed to the brutally raw cold, how I was forced to stand hours in the rain and snow which froze my hair. Another moment and I realized where I was, in the hospital room. I studied my face in the mirror and I saw that the inhumane conditions I suffered through had left their marks on me. I looked closely and saw that the left side of my head was swollen, my left eye was red, mostly closed. I could hardly see out of it. Touching the left side of my head, I felt the pain. The nurse gave me medication for my wounds. I soon learned that I was in a medical facility under American supervision. This was fortunate, for I did not trust German doctors, or any Germans, for that matter.

A shower was the first order of the day, then a shave. I had to get accustomed to a normal life which I had forgotten. It felt so good to be free, a freedom that had come to me as a gift. This was my new beginning. But then I felt a different kind of pain, that I was missing something terribly. Yes, I was missing my loved ones to share the happiness of my liberation. It was terrible to be so alone. I had to go on my new road, to adjust to a new life, a life without the people I loved and who loved me. My heart was filled with joy and sorrow.

I will never forget my first breakfast. On a tray in front of me were four pieces of warm toast, scrambled eggs, a cup of hot coffee, sugar, and a cup of milk. I was shaking with excitement and anticipation. So much food, and all for me! As soon as the nurses left the room I grabbed two pieces of toast and quickly put them under my pillow. The feeling of deprivation was still alive in me; I was afraid that tomorrow there would be no more food. The faces of the starving would not leave me in peace. My freedom had come too suddenly, events were moving too fast for me to adjust. For two weeks I kept bread under my pillow. I was no longer hungry but I still felt threatened by the possibility of starvation.

My second night in the hospital was sleepless, like the previous night. The wound on the left side of my head continued to throb, keeping me awake. When the morning came I looked out the window in amazement. It was beautiful—the mountains on the horizon, the sun shining through the breaks in the clouds, birds soaring in the morning mist. I felt alive again. This was spring, the first time in so many years that I could appreciate the wonders of nature. I felt my system recovering, as slowly I became human again. At that moment I felt tears running down my face. I was overwhelmed with the feeling of how good it was to be alive. I closed my eyes and the face of my friend Rabbi Lester appeared before me. His voice rang in my ears, "As long as you are alive, you have hope. The Almighty will help. Believe in Him." I shook my head, realizing that I was dreaming.

Chapter Sixteen

Adjusting to Freedom

My recovery proceeded slowly. It took awhile before I could come to terms with my new-found freedom, to put to rest the fear of imminent disaster. The feeling that I would starve to death gradually faded. I began to think more clearly. The pain in my legs subsided. I could move them. What a change! The only pain I felt was on the left side of my face. But as I enjoyed my physical healing, I started to suffer in a mental and moral sense. I was afraid to leave the hospital, knowing that I was living in Germany, whose soil was soaked with the blood of my loved ones. I regarded Germans as killers; they were the ones who murdered my family, my mother who gave me life. Never will I forget her loving face, covered with blood as she was hit repeatedly by gun-wielding SS men who forced her to walk to the cattle train on the way to the crematorium. I could still hear her calling me as the murderers dragged her away.

I was a man without a name, a nobody. A man with a present, but no past and an uncertain future. Where would I go to build a new tomorrow? For whom? Then the face of Helen, a beautiful young lady from Radom, appeared before me. It was the memory of Helen that had sustained me during my four years of horror. What happened to her? Is she still alive? Did she somehow survive the hell? The thought of Helen gave me the courage to face the future. I also started to entertain the hope that my brother Isaac had survived. I did not know what had happened to him after he was sent from Arbeitslager Szkolna to the extermination camp at Majdanek. I had so many questions, but at least I was beginning to address those uncertainties.

After a week in the hospital I started to walk. Slowly at first, and with the help of the medical staff. I knew the moment would soon come when I would have to leave my shelter which protected me from the hostile world outside. Finally, at the start of my second week in the hospital I went out of my room, into the world. I walked slowly, breathing the fresh air, looking around. Fussen was a pleasant little mountain city, undamaged by the war. It was very clean. I saw Germans, walking and talking to each other and smiling. I gazed at them and thought they looked like normal people. Are these the killers of millions of people? Standing there looking at them, I was afraid they would hit me. I saw a group of young men and women gathering nearby and I began to shake. In a panic, I ran back to the hospital, to my room. I fell on the bed, crying.

That night I could not sleep. That group of young people awakened memories of my life as a student in Warsaw. All my friends—they were gone, murdered with unfathomable cruelty. I was filled with sadness and despair. With tears in my eyes I recalled the time when I was with my brother and Helen and her brother Fishel. It was a few days before Isaac had been sent away to Majdanek. This was after the SS liquidated the small ghetto in my home town of Radom. I was sent to an Arbeitslager. The men and women were separated by a fence guarded by Ukrainians. I was in love with Helen and I ached to see her. The Ukrainian had orders to shoot anyone who tried to get past the fence. In order to see Helen I bribed the guards with a bottle of vodka I had smuggled into the *Arbeitslager*. This was one of the sweeter moments during those horrible times. Memories of Helen gave me the strength to go on, even when I was tormented by hunger and sickness. Sometimes when I was asleep I would call her name. Once my friend, Rabbi Lester, was lying close to me when I called out Helen's name in my sleep. My friend asked me who Helen was. I told him my story and how my physical pain was matched by my emotional anguish, wondering what had happened to Helen. "As long as you are alive, you have hope," the Rabbi comforted me. "The Almighty will help you. Believe in Him."

He was my spiritual guide, he built in me the will to fight and to survive, to believe in a tomorrow even as I was dying. This man never doubted the power of the Almighty, even in the last moments of his life. When beaten to death by an SS man his last words were, "SHEMAH ISRAEL," the unbroken belief in the power of Jehovah. Sitting in my hospital room, I said a few words of Kaddish (a prayer for the deceased) in memory of my friend. Once again, grief and sadness flooded my consciousness. Would I ever be free from the shadows of my past?

I realized I have to live with my sorrows and make the best of things if I was ever going to build a new life.

Chapter Seventeen

An Unsteady Recovery

Days passed and I got sick again. The swelling in my left eye grew worse so that I could not see out of it. The pain in the left side of my head grew more intense. I was suffering but I refused to see a German doctor. The Germans killed my family and as far as I was concerned at that time, the entire German nation was guilty. I spoke to an American doctor about this and he sent me to a friend of his, a Swiss doctor who was living in Fussen. I not only found a physician, I found a friend. He was someone I could talk to about my terrible past. I would sit in his office for hours talking about what I had endured. He was curing me physically as well as mentally. At that time I knew nothing about acupuncture, but I trusted this man. Every third day he would stick needles into the left side of my head near my left eye. Slowly the pain went away. This doctor, who was in his early seventies, gave me back my health. It has been fifty years and I have felt no pain in the area he treated. Wherever he is now, I will never forget him. He was my savior.

My physical wounds healed, and I began to gain weight, up from the 125 pounds when I was liberated. I was walking without help and I began to sleep at night, although not without horrifying dreams. I was not completely cured. Sometimes I would stop in the middle of a street, expecting something terrible to happen to me. The past will always be a part of me, I can never forget.

Following my hospitalization I lived in Germany, which made it more difficult to forget. For me, Germany was a cemetery, a graveyard for my beloved, and I longed to leave this place of slaughter. While walking in Fussen, I saw some elderly people passing by. I thought perhaps they had been the ones who murdered my parents. I am a man of peace and it never entered my mind to seek revenge, but I could not forgive the Germans. Years later I could not hate their children who had been born after the Holocaust. That generation must remember the mistakes of their parents and grandparents, to understand what hate and bigotry can do.

Epilogue

Dear reader, you came a long way with me. It was not easy to go back to my days filled with sorrows, to return to the most agonizing times of my life. I lost everything so dear to a human being. I nearly did not make it. As I sat down to write this book I thought deeply about how Judaism was able to withstand the Nazi onslaught. I remembered the liquidation of our ghetto in Radom when my father said to me, "Joseph, go save yourself. My place is with your brother. He is a cripple. He needs my help. You are young and strong. Go, before it will be too late." Until the last minute, we, the victims, behaved with dignity. My father did not forget his moral standard as the protector of his loved ones. Our moral code dictated that we should stand together to face the hostile world in which Jews lived. We survived the thousands of years of the Diaspora because we felt the power in the sense of belonging, the closeness of family, and most of all, the belief in the Almighty who gave us strength to overcome the darkest moments of our past. So many young men and women of our faith emerged from hiding and some returned from the partisans to rejoin their loved ones. The power of belonging was stronger than the fear of death.

Nevertheless, the pain of the past has not diminished. Writing about Jacob toward the end of the story triggered the memory of losing my family. This moment touched me so deeply that I suffered a nervous breakdown. Sitting at my typewriter, I suddenly saw the image of the SS beating my mother with my sister at her side. Something happened to me—I thought I was going crazy. Then suddenly, I lost hearing in my left ear. A terrible noise echoed on the left side of my head and I lost consciousness. When I came to I felt tears streaming down my face. I gazed upon the picture of my family which was hanging from the wall, and I began to shake uncontrollably. Haunted by memories of inhuman suffering, I could not write another word. It took four weeks to recover the ability to write again and to finish this book.

As I reflect on the nightmare of the Nazi years, I feel sadness, rage, and triumph. Sadness over what I have lost and rage over the degrading and cruel torture imposed on me and my fellow Jews. The Hitlerites robbed us of our property, our citizenship, and for too many, our right to exist. But try as they did with all the resources available, they failed to deprive us of our dignity. More than fifty years later survivors are telling their stories no matter how painful, recording for all generations the crimes and outrages committed by the so-called 'master race'.

For myself, the hour is growing late; I am compelled to follow the dictates of my teacher, Elie Wiesel, who directed me: "Write! That is your job—to recall and warn all humanity NEVER TO FORGET WHAT HAPPENED TO OUR PEOPLE. Recalling our tragedy will serve to demonstrate what bigotry and hate can do."

So, with great difficulty, I took up the ordeal of remembrance in hope that my grandchildren and all grandchildren, regardless of religion or race, will not suffer what my generation was forced to endure. The shadows of my tragic past have fallen on my children who had to grow up without uncles, aunts, cousins; they did not know what it meant to have grandparents. I therefore dedicate this book to the children of tomorrow who must never experience the unmitigated horror perpetrated against European Jewry.

Joseph Freeman's first meeting with his "Liberator" at Redlands High School in 1987.

An Afterword

It's Not So Easy:
Joseph Freeman's Memory-work

Late in the summer of 1994, I received a telephone call from Joseph Freeman. Aware of my teaching and writing about the Holocaust, this Jewish survivor asked me to read and comment on the autobiographical manuscript he had written. With some frequency, Holocaust survivors send me such requests. Each time I am moved by what I read, but for three reasons the impact of Joseph Freeman's words was especially strong.

First, Freeman uses language with the clarity, simplicity and compactness that identify a gifted writer. Second, his memoir was carefully researched. Drawing profoundly on his personal experience, Freeman had succeeded in doing even more because he had subtly contextualized his story within the larger history of the Holocaust's immense devastation. Third, some of Freeman's chapters provided glimpses into a part of the Holocaust's history that has been discussed much less—even in survivor testimony—than what happened, for example, to Jews in ghettos or camps. I refer to the infamous death marches that took place in the last months of World War II, well after the military tide had turned against Nazi Germany and its killing centers on Polish soil—Auschwitz-Birkenau among them—had been shut down and evacuated.

Especially with respect to Freeman's account of the death marches, however, I sensed that there was more to his story than he had told. I urged him to turn the glimpses into a more detailed narrative. He said he would do so in a second book.

Two years after Joseph Freeman contacted me, his first manuscript was published. He titled it *Job: The Story of a Holocaust Survivor*. As powerful as it is concise, that book is of lasting importance. Pleased as I was when its author sent me an inscribed copy, I was even more impressed when he handed me his second manuscript, the death-march sequel to *Job*, which became the book you have now been reading. *The Road to Hell: Recollections of the Nazi Death March* turns glimpses of too-little-studied dimensions of the Holocaust into a succinctly detailed narrative that shows how cruel and systematic, how brutal and unrelenting, the Third Reich's destruction of the European Jews turned out to be.

Grim though they are, Joseph Freeman's words create caring. For instance, his initial telephone call to me started to build friendship between us. That friendship brings him to my annual Holocaust class at Claremont McKenna College. When he speaks to the class, my students and I always notice two characteristics. First, in spite of the inhumanity he has experienced directly, there is Freeman's firm commitment to mend the world. Second, there is the phrase he often repeats: "It's not so easy." The phrase and the commitment belong together. To see how that connection works, reflect once more on *The Road to Hell.*

"It's not so easy"—when Joseph Freeman uses those words, he is doing what Holocaust scholar James E. Young calls *"memory-work."* Freeman's memory-work has at least two dimensions. First, it requires him to excavate what Ida Fink, another survivor-author, aptly named "the ruins of memory." To identify such work as hard and painful understates the case massively. Readers of *The Road to Hell* will surely grasp that point as we try to comprehend what Freeman's testimony has to do. That memory-work must not only recall catastrophe but bring it back to life in the present so that what happened can be described and analyzed. Horror experienced once must be relived—again and again. Even that mandate, however, is incomplete. For the required memory-work, description and analysis alone will not suffice. The description must be detailed and accurate, the analysis honest and truthful. Those requirements permit neither cheap optimism nor easy hope.

Second, Freeman's memory-work requires him to communicate what he experienced. But the communication-work is not so easy, because his audience can scarcely imagine what he tries to describe. My students and I, for example, do our best. We work to comprehend what we are hearing when Joseph Freeman speaks to us, but the more we listen, the more we realize how far his experience is removed from ours.

My students and I know that Freeman speaks the truth. We also know that we were not "there." Try as he might, Joseph Freeman cannot bridge completely the gulf that separates him from us. We come to understand how much he feels this gulf as he keeps telling us, "It's not so easy." What he means is that he wants so much for us to grasp what happened, even as he realizes that he cannot find the words to bridge the gap, for there are none that can do so completely. Yet, even though we cannot comprehend fully, perhaps our learning is deepest, our grasp as great as it can be, just when we see how much he struggles to make clear and vivid what we can only glimpse from afar. Thus, in spite of the difficulty of communication, and as *The Road to Hell* shows, the struggles of Joseph

Freeman's memory-work make connections that are unforgettable.

Having taught about the Holocaust for many years, I have discovered that the best learning strategies often involve concentrating, first, on small details, on events that are utterly particular but charged with intensity. As one explores how those details developed, how those events took place, they lead outward in spiraling concentric circles to wider historical perspectives. *The Road to Hell* is filled with memory-work, with particularities, of that kind.

One particular example in the book stands out more than any of the others. It involves hunger. For Jews who managed to stay alive during the Holocaust, hunger was a constant affliction, starvation an on-going threat. Hunger is an omnipresent theme in virtually all survivor testimony, but the intense particularity of Joseph Freeman's memory-work takes the description of hunger to depths of anguish unlike any others I have encountered in more than a quarter of a century of Holocaust research. Having read this book, you will know what I mean. It takes but a single word to trigger the recollection. The word is "vomit."

It's not so easy to recall that scene. It's not so easy for Joseph Freeman to remember it and to write about it. It's not so easy to try to fathom how that moment, that particularity, contains cruelty, devastation, and destructiveness that epitomize how the Holocaust—spawned from antisemitism and racism—wasted European Jewry and defaced humanity itself. With one word—vomit—Freeman sends us reeling into an abyss.

Remembering the Holocaust, survivor Jean Amery observed, "What happened, happened. But *that* it happened cannot be so easily accepted." Consequently, *The Road to Hell* does not—cannot—end with any simple resolution. Instead it draws to a close with a chapter called "An Unsteady Recovery." Although Freeman's readers have not shared his experiences directly, we can identify with that closing theme, for no one can read this book without feeling unsteady and yearning for recovery. Here, as feeling and yearning merge, Freeman's memory-work forges the link between "It's not so easy" and commitment to mend the world.

As my students and I observe when he speaks to us, Freeman's commitment to mend the world runs so deep precisely because his memory-work recalls disaster. Joseph Freeman has seen the worst. Therefore, the world must be mended. As Freeman understands and communicates so powerfully, that logic, that rhythm, that ethic governs the work that memory ought to do.

Joseph Freeman's memory-work in *The Road to Hell* makes us, his readers and listeners, Holocaust witnesses, too. It's not so easy, but by conferring that responsibility upon us, perhaps his memory-work and his commitment to mend the world encourage more memory-work that will make such mending grow.

John K. Roth, Ph.D.
Pitzer Professor of Philosophy
Claremont McKenna College

Notes

The first organized death march actually occurred much earlier in the war. On January 14, 1940 the SS forced eight hundred Jewish prisoners of war from the Polish army on a 62-mile march from Lublin to Biala Podlaska. Most of the prisoners died from the bitter cold and from Nazi persecution, and fewer than one hundred survived the ordeal. Early in the Pacific theater there was the notorious Bataan Death March, in which thousands of American and Filipino troops died at the hands of conquering Japanese forces. When Germany invaded the Soviet Union in the summer of 1941 thousands of Soviet prisoners of war were murdered while being transferred from the Ukraine and Belorussia. Finally, German troops and their collaborators forcibly evacuated tens of thousands of Jews from small towns and villages to large ghettos, and later from ghettos to concentration camps. Untold numbers of Jews were slaughtered on these forced marches.

The final camp to be evacuated was at Reichenau, in eastern Germany north of the Czech border.

See, Martin Brozart and Helmut Krausnick, *Anatomy of the SS State*, trans. Dorothy Lang and Marian Jackson (London, 1970), p. 249; and, Yehuda Bauer, "The Death-Marches, January-May 1945," *Modern Judaism* 3 (1983), pp. 1-21.

Glossary

AKTION - operation by the Nazis to humiliate, kill or to send to Jews in the ghettos to the extermination camps.

ARBEITSLAGER-SKOLNA - labor camp in Radom, Poland.

APPEL - counting of inmates at the extermination camps.

AUSCHWITZ - death camp in Poland.

DIASPORA - word used to identify Jews living outside the abate of Israel.

GROSS ROSEN - death camp in Germany.

HOLOCAUST - (SHO'AH, Hurban—destruction in Hebrew) the most tragic period of Diaspora history and modern marking as a whole.

KIDDUSH HASHEM - (sanctifying the name of God) Hebrew term that was used in postbiblical Jewish history to denote exemplary ethical conduct and that was applied to religious martyrdom.

KIELCE - a city in Poland not too far from Radom.

KAPO - a inmate supervising a group of prisoners in the concentration camp. In the ghettos, the Jewish police were supervising groups of people working.

LESTER, RABBI - a friend of Joseph in Schoemberg death camp.

MUNCHEN (Munich)- city in Bayern where Joseph lived after the liberation.

SCHOEMBERG - extermination camp in Germany where Joseph suffered.

STUTTGARD (Stuttgart) - a city inWittenberg, Germany not too far from Schoemberg death camp.

SCHLUTMAN CHAIM - a friend that Joseph met in death camp Spaiching.

SH'MA YISRAEL ADOMAI ELOHAYNU ADONAI ACHAD (HEAR, O ISRAEL: THE LORD OUR GOD, THE LORD IS ONE) translation of a prayer from Hebrew to English.

WARSZAWA (Warsaw) - capitol of Poland where Joseph studied before World War II.

Sources

Encyclopedia Judaica (Jerusalem , Israel)

Konninyn G. Feig, "Hitler's Death Camps: The Sanity of Madness," *Encyclopedia of the Holocaust* (New York: MacMillan).